Table of Contents

Introduction... 1
Chapter 1: Introduction to Dropshipping................. 5
Chapter 2: Choosing a Profitable Niche...................9
Chapter 3: Finding Reliable Suppliers and Products 13
Chapter 4: Setting Up Your Dropshipping Store... 17
Chapter 5: Managing Inventory and Fulfillment.... 22
Chapter 6: Pricing and Profitability Strategies...... 26
Chapter 7: Marketing and Driving Traffic to Your Store... 32
Chapter 8: Providing Excellent Customer Service 38
Chapter 9: Scaling Your Dropshipping Business.. 42
Chapter 10: Evaluating Performance and Continuous Improvement.......................................48

Introduction

Starting a dropshipping business is an exciting and potentially lucrative opportunity for entrepreneurs. With the surge in e-commerce and the increasing popularity of online shopping, dropshipping has emerged as a favored method for selling products without the need to maintain inventory or make an upfront investment in stock. This ultimate guide is designed to equip you with all the information and strategies you need to start and successfully run your own dropshipping business.

Dropshipping has transformed the way business is conducted by eliminating the need for traditional inventory management and order fulfillment. Instead of storing and shipping products yourself, you collaborate with suppliers who handle these tasks for you. This arrangement allows you to concentrate on marketing, customer service, and growing your business.

In this book, we will delve into essential topics such as choosing a profitable niche, finding reliable suppliers and products, setting up your dropshipping store, managing inventory and fulfillment, pricing and profitability strategies, marketing and driving traffic to your store, providing excellent customer service, scaling your dropshipping business, and evaluating performance for continuous improvement.

To begin with, selecting the right niche is crucial. It's about finding a market segment that is not only profitable but also something you are passionate about. This passion will drive your dedication and enthusiasm, making it easier to overcome challenges along the way.

Next, we'll explore how to find reliable suppliers. A good supplier is the backbone of a successful dropshipping business. You need suppliers who are dependable, offer quality products, and can ship promptly. Building strong relationships with your suppliers can lead to better terms and smoother operations.

Setting up your dropshipping store involves choosing the right platform and creating a user-friendly website. Your store should be visually appealing and easy to navigate. We'll guide you through the process of setting up your store, from selecting a domain name to designing the layout and integrating essential features.

Managing inventory and fulfillment is simplified in dropshipping, but it still requires careful coordination. We'll discuss how to track your orders, manage stock levels, and ensure that your customers receive their products on time. Efficient inventory management can prevent issues like stockouts and overstocking, which can impact customer satisfaction and profitability.

Pricing and profitability strategies are vital to ensure your business is competitive and profitable. We'll cover various pricing models and how to calculate your margins to make informed decisions. Understanding the financial aspects of your business will help you set prices that attract customers while ensuring you make a profit.

Marketing is the engine that drives traffic to your store. We'll explore different marketing channels, such as social media, search engine optimization (SEO), pay-per-click (PPC) advertising, and email marketing. Effective marketing strategies will help you reach your target audience and convert visitors into customers.

Providing excellent customer service is crucial for building a loyal customer base. We'll discuss best practices for handling inquiries, resolving issues, and creating a positive shopping experience. Happy customers are more likely to return and recommend your store to others.

As your business grows, scaling becomes a priority. We'll share tips on how to expand your product range, enter new markets, and automate processes to handle increased order volumes efficiently. Scaling your business requires strategic planning and the right tools to support your growth.

Finally, evaluating performance and continuous improvement are essential for long-term success. We'll guide you on how to measure key performance indicators (KPIs), analyze data, and make informed decisions to optimize your business operations continually.

By the end of this guide, you will have a comprehensive understanding of the dropshipping business model and all the necessary tools and knowledge to start your own successful venture. So, let's embark on this exciting journey into the world of dropshipping and discover how you can turn your entrepreneurial dreams into reality.

Chapter 1: Introduction to Dropshipping

In today's digital age, starting an online business has never been easier. One of the most popular methods of selling products without needing to keep an inventory or make an upfront investment in stock is dropshipping. This first chapter will give you a comprehensive understanding of what dropshipping is and how it can transform your entrepreneurial journey.

What is Dropshipping?

Dropshipping is a business model that lets entrepreneurs sell products to their customers without holding any inventory. Instead of purchasing products in bulk and storing them, you partner with suppliers who handle the order fulfillment for you. This means you don't need to worry about managing inventory, packaging, or shipping.

Here's a simple breakdown of how dropshipping works:

1. **Set Up Your Online Store:** You create an online store and list products available from suppliers.
2. **Customer Orders:** Customers visit your store and place orders for the products they want.
3. **Order Fulfillment:** You forward these

orders and customer details to the supplier.
4. **Direct Shipping:** The supplier packages and ships the products directly to your customers.
5. **Profit Margin:** You earn a profit from the difference between the price you charge your customers and the price you pay your supplier.

Advantages of Dropshipping

Dropshipping offers several key advantages for aspiring entrepreneurs:

1. Low Startup Costs

Unlike traditional retail businesses, dropshipping requires minimal upfront investment. You don't need to purchase large quantities of inventory or rent a physical store. Most of your expenses will be focused on building and marketing your online store.

2. Location Independence

With a dropshipping business, you can manage your store from anywhere in the world as long as you have an internet connection. This flexibility allows you to travel, work remotely, or explore new opportunities without being tied down to a specific location.

3. Wide Product Selection

Since you're not limited by physical inventory, you can offer a wide variety of products to your customers. You can source products from various suppliers and experiment with different niches to find what works best for your business.

4. Low Risk and Scalability

Dropshipping eliminates the risk of purchasing inventory upfront because you only pay for products once you've made a sale. This makes it easier for entrepreneurs to test different products and scale their business quickly without the fear of being stuck with unsold inventory.

Conclusion

Dropshipping is an attractive business model that offers low startup costs, location independence, a wide product selection, and low risk. This chapter has provided you with a solid foundation on what dropshipping is and the advantages it presents for entrepreneurs.

In the next chapter, we'll dive deeper into the process of choosing a profitable niche, helping you take the first step towards building your successful dropshipping business.

Chapter 2: Choosing a Profitable Niche

Starting a dropshipping business is an exciting venture, and one of the most critical steps to ensure your success is choosing a profitable niche. Essentially, a niche is a specific segment of the market that caters to a particular group of customers with unique needs and preferences. Selecting a niche that is not only profitable but also aligns with your interests can significantly impact your business's success. Let's delve into why this is so important and how you can go about identifying the perfect niche for your dropshipping store.

Why Choosing a Niche is Important

Focusing on a niche market is essential for several reasons:

1. **Less Competition:** By targeting a specific niche, you can reduce the amount of competition you face. This is because you're not just another generic store selling a broad range of products. Instead, you're offering something unique that stands out, which makes it easier to differentiate yourself from other online retailers.
2. **Higher Conversion Rates:** When you specialize in a specific niche, you become an expert in that area. This

expertise builds trust with your customers, resulting in higher conversion rates. People are more likely to buy from a store that understands their needs and offers tailored product solutions.
3. **Repeat Customers:** Catering to a niche market helps you build a loyal customer base. When customers have a positive experience with your products, they are more likely to return. This leads to repeat purchases and increases the lifetime value of your customers.

Identifying a Profitable Niche

Finding the right niche may seem daunting, but with thorough research and analysis, you can discover profitable opportunities. Here are some steps to help you identify a niche that works for you:

1. **Passion and Interest:** Begin by brainstorming topics you are passionate about or knowledgeable in. Think about your hobbies, interests, and areas of expertise. Choosing a niche that you enjoy will make your business journey more enjoyable and provide you with a deeper understanding of your customers' needs.
2. **Market Demand:** Once you have a list of potential niches, research their

market demand. Look for products that have a steady and growing demand. Tools like Google Trends, keyword research, and industry reports can help you assess the popularity and demand for your potential niche.
3. **Competition Analysis:** Evaluate the level of competition within your chosen niche. While a little competition is healthy, you need to ensure there is room for your business to thrive. Analyze your competitors' strengths and weaknesses, identify gaps in their product offerings, and find ways to differentiate yourself.
4. **Profitability:** Consider the profitability of your niche. Look for products with reasonable profit margins and the potential for upselling or cross-selling. Calculate the costs involved in sourcing and shipping products to ensure your business remains profitable.
5. **Target Audience:** Understand your target audience's demographics, interests, and buying behaviors. This knowledge will help you tailor your marketing strategies and product offerings specifically to them, increasing your chances of success.

Final Thoughts

Choosing a profitable niche is a foundational

step in building a successful dropshipping business. By focusing on a specific market segment, you can differentiate yourself, attract a loyal customer base, and increase conversion rates. Remember to consider your passions and interests, assess market demand, analyze competition, and ensure profitability. With proper research and a well-chosen niche, you set yourself up for success in the dropshipping industry.

In the next chapter, we'll discuss how to find reliable suppliers and high-quality products to ensure your business runs smoothly and meets your customers' expectations.

Chapter 3: Finding Reliable Suppliers and Products

Finding reliable suppliers and high-quality products is a crucial step in launching and maintaining a successful dropshipping business. The quality of your products and the dependability of your suppliers can directly impact customer satisfaction, your brand's reputation, and your overall profitability. Let's dive into how you can effectively find and vet suppliers, diversify your supplier base, and evaluate products to ensure your business thrives.

Researching and Vetting Suppliers

When you start looking for suppliers, it's essential to conduct thorough research and vetting. This ensures they are reliable, trustworthy, and can meet your business needs. Here are some steps to follow:

1. **Look for Established Suppliers:** Seek out suppliers who have been in the business for a while and have a good reputation within the industry. Established suppliers are more likely to have experience, reliable processes, and a proven track record of delivering quality products.
2. **Check Supplier Reviews and Ratings:**

Look for reviews and ratings of suppliers online. Platforms like Alibaba, Oberlo, and AliExpress have built-in rating systems that can provide valuable insights into a supplier's performance and reliability.
3. **Request Samples:** Request samples from potential suppliers to assess the quality of their products. This will help you ensure that the products meet your standards and will satisfy your customers.
4. **Communicate and Ask Questions:** Reach out to suppliers directly and ask them questions about their processes, lead times, and any specific requirements you may have. Their responsiveness and willingness to communicate can be a good indicator of their professionalism and reliability.

Diversifying Your Supplier Base

Relying on a single supplier can be risky because it leaves your business vulnerable to supply chain disruptions. To mitigate this risk, consider diversifying your supplier base by working with multiple suppliers. Here are a few reasons why diversifying your suppliers is beneficial:

1. **Backup Options:** Having multiple suppliers allows you to quickly switch to

an alternative if one supplier experiences issues with production, shipping, or quality control.
2. **Competitive Pricing:** Working with multiple suppliers gives you the opportunity to compare prices and negotiate better deals. This can help you maintain competitive pricing for your customers.
3. **Product Variety:** Different suppliers may offer a wider range of products, allowing you to expand your product catalog and cater to the diverse preferences of your target market.

Product Research and Evaluation

In addition to finding reliable suppliers, it's important to research and evaluate the products you will be selling. Here are some tips for finding profitable and high-quality products:

1. **Analyze Market Trends:** Use tools like Google Trends and social media platforms to identify current market trends and popular product categories. This can help you determine which products are in demand and have the potential for high sales.
2. **Conduct Competitor Analysis:** Research your competitors to identify their top-selling products and pricing

strategies. This can give you insights into what products are performing well in the market.
3. **Consider Product Quality and Reviews:** Look for products with positive customer reviews and high ratings. Quality products lead to satisfied customers, positive reviews, and repeat business.
4. **Evaluate Profit Margins:** Calculate your potential profit margins for each product by considering the cost of the product, shipping fees, and any additional expenses. Focus on products that offer a reasonable profit margin while still being competitive in the market.

By thoroughly researching and vetting suppliers and products, you can ensure that you are working with reliable partners and offering high-quality products to your customers. This will help establish trust, build a strong brand reputation, and contribute to the long-term success of your dropshipping business.

Next, we will discuss how to set up your dropshipping store.

Chapter 4: Setting Up Your Dropshipping Store

Setting up your dropshipping store is a crucial step in starting your online business. It's important to create a professional and user-friendly website that showcases your products and encourages visitors to make a purchase. In this chapter, we will guide you through the process of setting up your dropshipping store.

Choosing an E-commerce Platform

When it comes to setting up your dropshipping store, choosing the right e-commerce platform is essential. There are various platforms available, each with its own features and advantages. Here are some popular e-commerce platforms that you can consider:

1. **Shopify:** Shopify is one of the most popular e-commerce platforms for dropshipping businesses. It offers an easy-to-use interface, customizable themes, and a wide range of apps and integrations to enhance your store's functionality.
2. **WooCommerce:** If you're already using WordPress, WooCommerce is a great option. It seamlessly integrates with WordPress and provides flexibility in terms of design and functionality.

3. **BigCommerce:** BigCommerce is known for its scalability and robust features. It offers a range of built-in marketing tools and integrates with various payment gateways.
4. **Magento:** Magento is a powerful and feature-rich platform, ideal for large-scale businesses. It offers advanced customization options and can handle high traffic volumes.

Consider your business needs, technical expertise, and budget when choosing an e-commerce platform.

Designing Your Store

Once you have selected your e-commerce platform, it's time to design your store. A visually appealing and user-friendly website can greatly impact your customers' experience and increase conversion rates. Here are some design considerations:

1. **Choose a Clean and Professional Theme:** Select a theme that aligns with your brand identity. Customize the colors, fonts, and images to create a cohesive and branded look.
2. **Ensure Mobile Responsiveness:** With the increasing use of mobile devices, it's crucial to provide a seamless experience across different screen

sizes.
3. **Optimize Loading Speed:** A slow-loading website can deter customers. Optimize your images and minimize unnecessary scripts to improve performance.
4. **Create Clear Navigation Menus:** Make it easy for customers to find what they're looking for with intuitive product categories.
5. **Use High-Quality Product Images and Descriptions:** These should accurately represent your products and highlight their unique selling points.
6. **Implement a User-Friendly and Secure Checkout Process:** Simplify the checkout steps and offer popular payment options to increase customer trust and satisfaction.

Setting Up Payment Gateways
To accept payments from your customers, you need to set up payment gateways. Payment gateways allow you to securely process credit card transactions and other methods of payment. Popular payment gateways include PayPal, Stripe, and Authorize.Net. When choosing a payment gateway, consider factors such as transaction fees, supported countries, ease of integration with your e-commerce platform, and customer trust and familiarity with the gateway.

Integrating with Dropshipping Suppliers
Once your store is set up, you need to integrate it with your chosen dropshipping suppliers. This integration allows for smooth order fulfillment and inventory management. Many e-commerce platforms offer built-in integrations with popular dropshipping suppliers, making the process easier. Make sure to provide your supplier with the necessary access and information to fulfill orders on your behalf. This includes the ability to access order details, shipping addresses, and customer information.

Testing and Launching Your Store
Before launching your store to the public, it's crucial to thoroughly test its functionality. Test the browsing experience, add products to the cart, and simulate the entire checkout process. This testing phase helps identify any issues and allows you to make necessary adjustments before going live.

Once you are confident in the functionality of your store, it's time to launch it to the public. Make sure to promote your store through social media, email marketing, and other relevant channels to generate traffic and increase brand visibility.

Congratulations! You have successfully set up your dropshipping store. In the next chapter, we will discuss how to manage inventory and fulfillment efficiently.

Chapter 5: Managing Inventory and Fulfillment

Managing inventory and fulfillment is absolutely critical when running a successful dropshipping business. In this chapter, we'll dive into the essential strategies and best practices for effectively managing your inventory and ensuring timely fulfillment of orders. Let's get started!

Understanding Inventory Management

In a traditional retail business, inventory management involves purchasing, storing, and tracking stock levels. However, in a dropshipping business, things work a bit differently. You don't have physical control over the inventory since your suppliers handle the storage and shipping of products directly to your customers. While this means you don't have to worry about storing products, it's still crucial to keep track of your suppliers' inventory levels. This helps prevent overselling and keeps your customers happy.

Implementing Inventory Tracking Systems

To manage your inventory effectively, consider using inventory tracking systems or software that integrates with your dropshipping platform. These tools can automate the process of tracking stock levels and updating your product listings accordingly. They can also alert you when certain products are running low or out of stock.

When choosing an inventory tracking system, make sure it integrates seamlessly with your e-commerce platform and provides real-time data on product availability. This will help you stay organized and ensure a smooth order fulfillment process.

Setting Realistic Expectations

Setting realistic expectations with your customers is key to successful inventory management in dropshipping. Since you don't have direct control over the inventory, there may be times when a product becomes out of stock or unavailable. To avoid disappointing your customers, clearly communicate the estimated shipping times on your website and during the checkout process.

Be transparent about any potential delays or backorders and provide regular updates to customers when necessary. This approach helps build trust and manage customer expectations effectively.

Streamlining Order Fulfillment

Order fulfillment involves receiving and processing customer orders, coordinating with your suppliers, and ensuring that products are shipped to customers promptly. Here are some key strategies to streamline your order fulfillment process:

Automate Order Processing

Instead of manually forwarding orders to your suppliers, consider automating the order processing system. Most e-commerce platforms offer integrations with suppliers, allowing orders to be automatically sent to them once a customer makes a purchase on your website. By automating this process, you can save time and reduce the chances of errors or delays in forwarding orders to suppliers, ensuring a seamless and efficient fulfillment process.

Track Order Status and Delivery

Once an order has been placed, it's crucial to track its status and delivery to keep your customers informed. Partnering with shipping carriers that provide tracking services can help you provide real-time updates to customers regarding the progress of their orders. Integrating order tracking systems into your e-commerce platform or using third-party tracking software can simplify this process. Make sure to provide customers with tracking numbers and clear instructions on how to track their shipments.

Ensure Quality Control

As a dropshipper, you are responsible for the overall customer experience, including the quality of the products shipped. While you rely on your suppliers for fulfillment, it's essential to establish quality control measures. This includes regularly reviewing supplier performance, inspecting product samples, and promptly addressing any customer complaints. Maintaining high-quality standards will help you build a positive reputation, increase customer satisfaction, and reduce the number of returns or refunds.

Conclusion

Managing inventory and fulfillment is a crucial aspect of running a dropshipping business. By implementing effective inventory tracking systems, setting realistic expectations, and streamlining the order fulfillment process, you can ensure a smooth and efficient operation. Remember, maintaining clear communication with customers and suppliers is key to providing a positive experience and building a thriving dropshipping business.

Chapter 6: Pricing and Profitability Strategies

Setting the right prices for your products is a crucial aspect of running a successful dropshipping business. You need to cover your costs and make a profit, but you also want to stay competitive in the market. In this chapter, we'll delve into various pricing and profitability strategies that can help you achieve these goals.

Determining Costs

Before you can set your prices, it's essential to have a clear understanding of all your costs. This includes not only the wholesale price of the products but also any additional fees associated with running your business. Here are some key costs to consider:

Product Cost:

1. This is the price you pay your suppliers for each product. Be sure to factor in the cost of shipping, packaging, and any additional fees that might apply.

Transaction Fees:

2. Platforms like Shopify or PayPal may

charge transaction fees when processing payments. These fees can vary, so it's important to include them in your pricing strategy.

Marketing Costs:

3. Consider any expenses related to advertising, social media promotions, and search engine optimization (SEO) efforts. These costs are crucial for driving traffic and generating sales.

Operating Costs:

4. Include expenses related to website maintenance, hosting fees, software subscriptions, and customer support.

Once you have a clear picture of your costs, you can proceed with setting your prices.

Pricing Strategies

When it comes to pricing your products in a dropshipping business, there are several strategies to consider. Each strategy has its own advantages and may work better depending on your target audience and niche. Here are a few popular pricing strategies:

Competitive Pricing:

1. Setting your prices in line with your competitors can help you remain competitive in your market. Conduct market research to determine the average price range for similar products and align your prices accordingly. However, ensure that your profit margins are still sufficient to cover your costs and make a profit.

Value-Based Pricing:

2. This strategy involves pricing your products based on the perceived value they offer to customers. Focus on the unique features, benefits, or quality of your products and set your prices accordingly. This strategy works well when targeting a niche market that values specific attributes or experiences.

Penetration Pricing:

3. This strategy involves setting lower prices than your competitors to attract customers and gain market share. It can be particularly effective when starting out or when trying to enter a highly competitive market. However, make sure to assess your profit margins and

have a plan to gradually increase prices over time.

Bundling and Upselling:

4. Offering bundled products or upselling additional items can increase the average order value and boost profitability. For example, you can bundle related products together at a slightly discounted price or offer premium versions of products at a higher price point.

Monitoring and Adjusting Prices

Pricing is not a set-it-and-forget-it strategy. It's important to regularly monitor and adjust your prices based on various factors such as product demand, competition, and market trends. Here are a few tips to help you effectively manage your pricing:

Track the Competition:

1. Keep an eye on your competitors' prices and adjust accordingly. If they lower their prices, you may need to review your own pricing strategy to remain competitive.

Analyze Customer Behavior:

2. Monitor how customers respond to different price points. Conduct A/B testing with different pricing structures to gauge customer preferences and optimize your pricing strategy.

Consider Seasonality:

3. Some products may have fluctuating demand based on seasonality or trends. Adjust your prices accordingly during peak seasons to maximize sales and profitability.

Offer Discounts and Promotions:

4. Use discounts, sales, and limited-time offers strategically to drive sales and create a sense of urgency among customers. However, be mindful of your profit margins and ensure that discounts are still profitable.

Regularly Review Costs:

5. Keep track of any changes in costs, including supplier prices, shipping fees, and additional expenses. Adjust your prices if necessary to maintain profitability.

Conclusion

Pricing is a critical aspect of running a successful dropshipping business. By understanding your costs, implementing strategic pricing strategies, and regularly reviewing and adjusting your prices, you can maximize profitability while remaining competitive in the market. Remember to analyze customer behavior, track the competition, and consider seasonality when setting your prices. With careful planning and continuous monitoring, you'll be well-equipped to navigate the complexities of pricing in the dropshipping industry.

Chapter 7: Marketing and Driving Traffic to Your Store

Marketing is the lifeblood of any business, and dropshipping is no exception. To thrive in the dropshipping world, you need to actively promote your store and drive traffic to it. In this chapter, we'll explore various marketing strategies and tactics that can help you attract potential customers and boost your sales.

Creating a Marketing Plan

Before jumping into specific marketing strategies, it's crucial to create a comprehensive marketing plan. This plan will serve as your roadmap, ensuring that your marketing efforts are aligned with your business goals. Here's what you should include:

Target Audience
First, identify your target audience. Who are they? What are their demographics, interests, and buying behaviors? Understanding your ideal customers will help you tailor your marketing messages effectively.

Marketing Channels
Decide which marketing channels will best reach your target audience. Common channels for dropshipping businesses include social

media, email marketing, influencer partnerships, content marketing, and paid advertising. Think about where your audience spends their time and focus your efforts there.

Marketing Budget
Set a budget for your marketing activities. This will help you allocate resources efficiently and measure the return on investment (ROI) for your campaigns.

Goals and Key Performance Indicators (KPIs)
Define clear goals for your marketing efforts, such as increasing website traffic, generating leads, or improving conversion rates. Establish KPIs to measure your success and regularly analyze your performance against these metrics.

Social Media Marketing

Social media platforms offer incredible opportunities to connect with potential customers, build brand awareness, and drive traffic to your store. Here are some tips to make the most of social media:

Choose the Right Platforms
Focus on the social media platforms where your target audience is most active. For instance, if your target audience consists of young adults, platforms like Instagram and TikTok might be more effective.

Create Engaging Content
Develop a content strategy that resonates with your audience's interests and preferences. Share engaging content, such as product showcases, tutorials, customer testimonials, and behind-the-scenes glimpses. Encourage interaction through comments, likes, shares, and contests.

Build Relationships with Influencers
Collaborate with influencers who align with your niche and have a significant following. Influencers can help you reach a broader audience and boost brand visibility. Consider sponsored posts, product reviews, or affiliate partnerships with influencers.

Email Marketing

Email marketing is a powerful tool for nurturing relationships with customers and driving sales. Here's how to leverage it effectively:

Build an Email List
Collect email addresses from website visitors by offering incentives like exclusive discounts, freebies, or valuable content. Use lead capture tools and strategically placed forms on your website to encourage sign-ups.

Segment Your Email List
Divide your email list into segments based on demographics, purchase history, and

engagement levels. This allows you to send targeted and relevant emails to each segment.

Personalize Your Emails
Personalize your emails by addressing subscribers by name and tailoring content to their preferences. Personalized emails typically have higher open and click-through rates.

Send Regular Newsletters and Promotions
Keep your subscribers engaged with regular newsletters that include product updates, helpful tips, and exclusive offers. Use discounts or limited-time promotions to incentivize purchases.

Content Marketing

Content marketing involves creating and sharing valuable content to attract and engage your audience. Here's how to use it for your dropshipping business:

Create a Blog
Start a blog on your website or a separate blogging platform. Write informative articles related to your niche, such as product guides, how-to tutorials, and industry news. Share your blog posts on social media and through email marketing to increase visibility.

Guest Blogging
Write guest posts for other relevant blogs or

websites in your industry. This can help establish you as an expert in your niche and drive traffic to your store through backlinks.

Video Marketing
Create video content like product demos, tutorials, or informative videos related to your niche. Publish these videos on platforms like YouTube and share them on your website and social media channels.

Paid Advertising

Paid advertising can be an effective way to quickly drive traffic to your store. Consider using platforms like Google Ads, Facebook Ads, or Instagram Ads. Here are some tips for successful paid advertising:

Set a Budget
Determine your budget for paid advertising and set daily or monthly limits. Start with a smaller budget and gradually increase it based on the results you achieve.

Target Specific Keywords and Audiences
Choose the right keywords and demographics to target in your campaigns. Conduct thorough keyword research and use the audience targeting options provided by advertising platforms.

Create Compelling Ad Copy

Write persuasive ad copy that highlights the unique selling points of your products. Use compelling visuals and clear calls-to-action (CTAs) to entice users to click on your ads.

Analyze and Optimize
Regularly monitor the performance of your paid advertising campaigns and make data-driven optimizations. Adjust your targeting, ad copy, and budget based on the KPIs you set in your marketing plan.

Conclusion

Marketing and driving traffic to your dropshipping store are essential components of building a successful business. By creating a comprehensive marketing plan and utilizing strategies like social media marketing, email marketing, content marketing, and paid advertising, you can attract potential customers, generate sales, and establish your brand in the competitive dropshipping market. Remember to track your efforts, measure the results, and continuously optimize your strategies for the best possible outcomes.

Chapter 8: Providing Excellent Customer Service

In any business, especially in dropshipping, providing excellent customer service is essential for success. Happy customers lead to higher sales, repeat purchases, and positive word-of-mouth advertising. In this chapter, we'll explore strategies and best practices for providing exceptional customer service in your dropshipping business.

1. Prompt and Clear Communication

One of the most important aspects of customer service is prompt and clear communication. When customers reach out with questions or concerns, it's crucial to respond quickly and with accurate information. Aim to reply to customer inquiries within 24 hours or sooner if possible. If there are delays or issues with order processing or shipping, inform customers immediately and provide regular updates on the status of their orders. Clear and efficient communication builds trust and confidence in your business.

2. Be Knowledgeable About Your Products

Customers often have specific questions about the products you offer. It's important to be knowledgeable about the features, specifications, and benefits of the products you sell. Take the time to familiarize yourself with the products so you can provide accurate and helpful information. This knowledge not only helps instill confidence in your customers but also showcases your expertise in your niche.

3. Handle Returns and Refunds Gracefully

In the dropshipping business, returns and refunds are inevitable. It's essential to have a clear and fair return policy in place. Make sure to communicate this policy clearly on your website so customers are aware of the process for returning or exchanging products. When handling returns or refunds, address customer concerns promptly and in a professional, courteous manner. Providing a smooth and hassle-free return experience leaves a positive impression on customers.

4. Personalize the Customer Experience

One way to stand out in the dropshipping business is by personalizing the customer experience. Address customers by their names in email communications and provide personalized product recommendations based on their purchase history or browsing behavior. This personal touch can make customers feel valued and appreciated.

5. Actively Seek Customer Feedback

Regularly seeking customer feedback is an important part of providing excellent customer service. Encourage customers to leave reviews and ratings on your website or third-party platforms. Additionally, consider sending follow-up emails or surveys to customers after they have made a purchase, asking for their opinions on their shopping experience. Use this feedback to identify areas for improvement and make necessary adjustments to enhance the customer experience.

6. Train and Empower Your Support Team

If you have a support team or customer service representatives, it's crucial to train them effectively. Provide them with the necessary knowledge about your products, policies, and processes so they can assist customers with their inquiries or issues. Empower your support team to make decisions and resolve customer concerns independently, within the guidelines you have set. This enables them to provide efficient and satisfactory solutions to customer problems.

7. Foster a Positive Brand Image

Consistently delivering exceptional customer service contributes to building a positive brand image. Customers who have a positive experience with your dropshipping business are more likely to recommend your store to others and become repeat customers themselves. Going above and beyond in terms of customer service helps differentiate your brand from competitors and positions your business as a leader in your niche.

Conclusion

Providing excellent customer service is a key differentiator for a successful dropshipping business. By prioritizing prompt communication, product knowledge, smooth returns and refunds, personalized experiences, customer feedback, well-trained support teams, and fostering a positive brand image, you can build strong relationships with customers and establish your business as a trusted and reliable source for their needs. Remember, customer satisfaction and loyalty should always be at the forefront of your dropshipping operations.

Chapter 9: Scaling Your Dropshipping Business

Scaling your dropshipping business is essential for achieving long-term success and profitability. It involves expanding your operations, increasing sales volume, and reaching a broader customer base. In this chapter, we'll dive into key strategies and tactics to effectively scale your dropshipping business.

Streamline and Automate Processes

As your business grows, it becomes crucial to streamline and automate various processes to handle the increased workload efficiently. Here are some areas where you can focus on automation:

1. **Order Processing:** Invest in software or systems that can automate the process of forwarding orders to your suppliers. This will save you time and reduce the risk of errors.
2. **Inventory Management:** Implement an inventory management system that can track stock levels in real-time and automatically update your website accordingly. This helps you avoid overselling products and improves order fulfillment.
3. **Customer Support:** Consider using

chatbots or automated messaging systems to handle basic customer inquiries. This frees up your time and resources to focus on more complex customer issues.
4. **Marketing Automation:** Utilize email marketing automation tools to send personalized emails to your customers at different stages of the customer journey. This drives repeat purchases and increases customer loyalty.

Expand Product Offering

Once your dropshipping business is well-established, consider expanding your product range to attract a wider customer base and increase sales. Here are some strategies to expand your product offering:

1. **Market Research:** Conduct thorough market research to identify new product opportunities within your niche. Look for complementary or related products that your existing customers may be interested in.
2. **Supplier Research:** Find new suppliers that offer the products you want to add to your inventory. Ensure that they are reliable and can meet your quality and fulfillment requirements.
3. **Test New Products:** Before adding new products to your website, consider

testing them with a small batch order to gauge customer demand and profitability.
4. **Monitor Performance:** Regularly monitor the performance of new products to determine their popularity and profitability. Make data-driven decisions about whether to continue stocking these products or remove them from your inventory.

Optimize Marketing Strategies

To scale your dropshipping business, you need to adopt effective marketing strategies to attract more customers and increase sales. Here are some strategies to consider:

1. **Paid Advertising:** Allocate a portion of your budget to paid advertising channels such as Google Ads, Facebook Ads, or influencer marketing. Test different ad formats and audiences to optimize your return on investment.
2. **Search Engine Optimization (SEO):** Optimize your website and product pages for search engines to improve your organic rankings. Focus on relevant keywords, high-quality product descriptions, and a user-friendly website design.
3. **Social Media Marketing:** Leverage social media platforms to engage with

your target audience, share valuable content, and promote your products. Use a mix of organic posts and paid ads to reach a wider audience.
4. **Email Marketing:** Develop an email marketing strategy to nurture your existing customers and drive repeat purchases. Segment your email list based on customer preferences and send personalized offers and promotions.

Strategic Partnerships

Consider building strategic partnerships with other businesses that align with your target audience and niche. Here are some partnership ideas to explore:

1. **Influencer Collaborations:** Collaborate with influencers or bloggers who have a significant following within your niche. They can promote your products and introduce your brand to a new audience.
2. **Cross-Promotion:** Partner with complementary businesses to cross-promote each other's products or offer bundled deals. This can help you reach a wider customer base and increase sales.
3. **Affiliate Marketing:** Set up an affiliate program where individuals or businesses can earn a commission for

referring customers to your store. This incentivizes others to promote your products and drive sales.
4. **Wholesale or B2B Partnerships:** Explore opportunities to sell your products wholesale to other businesses or B2B customers. This can be a profitable way to scale your business and increase distribution.

Monitor Key Metrics and Analytics

As you scale your dropshipping business, it's important to closely monitor key metrics and analytics to evaluate performance and make informed decisions. Some metrics to consider tracking include:

1. **Conversion Rate:** Measure the percentage of website visitors who make a purchase. A higher conversion rate indicates an effective marketing and sales strategy.
2. **Customer Acquisition Cost (CAC):** Calculate the expense required to acquire a new customer. This metric helps you evaluate the effectiveness of your marketing efforts.
3. **Average Order Value (AOV):** Determine the average amount customers spend per order. Increasing AOV can significantly boost revenue.
4. **Customer Lifetime Value (CLTV):**

Estimate the total revenue a customer generates over their lifetime. Focus on retaining and nurturing existing customers to increase CLTV.
5. **Return on Advertising Spend (ROAS):** Analyze the effectiveness of your advertising campaigns by comparing the revenue generated to the amount spent on advertising.

By regularly monitoring these metrics, you can identify areas of improvement and make strategic decisions to further scale your dropshipping business.

Conclusion

Scaling your dropshipping business requires careful planning, optimization, and continuous improvement. By streamlining processes, expanding your product offering, optimizing marketing strategies, building strategic partnerships, and monitoring key metrics, you can successfully scale your business and reach new heights of success and profitability. Remember to adapt your strategies as your business grows and continue to provide excellent customer service to maintain customer satisfaction.

Chapter 10: Evaluating Performance and Continuous Improvement

Tracking key metrics and evaluating the performance of your dropshipping business is crucial for making informed decisions and ensuring long-term success. In this chapter, we will explore the various metrics you should monitor and strategies for continuous improvement that will help you optimize your operations and grow your business.

Monitoring Key Metrics

To effectively evaluate the performance of your dropshipping business, it's important to track key metrics that provide insights into your customers, finances, and marketing efforts. Here are some essential metrics to monitor:

Conversion Rate:

1. The conversion rate measures the percentage of website visitors who make a purchase. It helps you understand the effectiveness of your marketing efforts and the performance of your website in driving sales. A high conversion rate indicates that your website is compelling and user-friendly, encouraging visitors to become

customers.

Customer Acquisition Cost (CAC):

2. CAC measures the amount of money you spend to acquire a new customer. This includes expenses on marketing campaigns, advertising, and other customer acquisition strategies. Monitoring your CAC helps you assess the efficiency of your marketing budget and find ways to optimize it. Lowering your CAC while maintaining or increasing sales is a key indicator of efficient marketing.

Average Order Value (AOV):

3. AOV calculates the average amount spent by a customer per order. Increasing your AOV is a key strategy to boost revenue without necessarily acquiring more customers. You can achieve this by focusing on cross-selling, upselling, or offering bundle deals, encouraging customers to spend more per order.

Customer Lifetime Value (CLV):

4. CLV is the predicted value of a customer over their lifetime of engagement with your business. Understanding CLV helps you gauge the long-term profitability of your customers and guides decisions related to customer retention and loyalty programs. Higher CLV indicates that your customers are satisfied and likely to make repeat purchases.

Return on Advertising Spend (ROAS):

5. ROAS measures the revenue generated for every dollar spent on advertising. It helps you assess the effectiveness of your advertising campaigns and optimize your ad spending. A high ROAS means you're getting a good return on your advertising investment, which is crucial for scaling your business profitably.

Continuous Improvement Strategies

Continuous improvement is essential for the growth and success of your dropshipping business. Here are some strategies to consider:

Analyze Performance Data:

1. Regularly review and analyze your performance data to identify trends, patterns, and areas for improvement. Use tools like Google Analytics, Excel spreadsheets, or specialized analytics platforms to track and analyze your metrics. This data-driven approach helps you make informed decisions and refine your strategies.

Set Clear Goals:

2. Define clear goals and key performance indicators (KPIs) that align with your business objectives. These goals can relate to revenue, customer acquisition, order fulfillment, or customer satisfaction. Regularly monitor your progress towards these goals and adjust your strategies as needed to stay on track.

Implement A/B Testing:

3. A/B testing involves creating two variations of a webpage, advertisement, or email campaign and comparing their performance to determine which version performs better. Test different elements such as headlines, images, colors, calls-to-action, or pricing to optimize

conversions and improve overall performance.

Improve Website User Experience:

4. Focus on providing an intuitive and user-friendly experience for your website visitors. Optimize your website's loading speed, navigation, and mobile responsiveness. A seamless and enjoyable browsing experience can improve customer satisfaction and increase conversions.

Optimize Product Descriptions and Images:

5. Craft compelling product descriptions and use high-quality images to convey the value and features of your products. Ensure that your product descriptions are accurate, detailed, and persuasive. High-quality images that showcase products from multiple angles can enhance the buying experience for customers.

Engage with Customer Feedback:

6. Actively seek and listen to customer feedback. Encourage customers to provide reviews, ratings, and

testimonials. Use customer feedback to improve your products, customer service, and overall user experience. Address any issues or complaints promptly and professionally to maintain a positive relationship with your customers.

Stay Updated with Market Trends:

7. Continuously monitor and adapt to changing market trends and customer preferences. Stay informed about new products, technologies, and industry developments. Conduct regular competitor analysis to stay ahead of the game and identify opportunities for improvement and differentiation.

Regularly Review and Update Marketing Strategies:

8. Evaluate and adjust your marketing strategies based on their performance and ROI. Experiment with different marketing channels, messaging, and audience targeting to identify the most effective strategies for driving traffic and sales. Stay up-to-date with the latest digital marketing trends and tactics to keep your marketing efforts fresh and

effective.

By consistently monitoring your key metrics and implementing strategies for continuous improvement, you can optimize the performance of your dropshipping business, increase customer satisfaction, and drive long-term success. Remember, success in dropshipping requires adaptability, innovation, and a commitment to delivering exceptional value to your customers. Keep refining your approach, and you'll be well on your way to building a thriving dropshipping business.

www.ingramcontent.com/pod-product-compliance
Lightning Source LLC
Chambersburg PA
CBHW071221240526
45470CB00018B/2096